5 MINUTES CHRISTMAS DEVOTIONALS FOR KIDS

A 31-Day Inspirational Journey for Children, Plus Winter Wonder Family Games and Bonding Moments

★ 2024 ★

Jeremiah Christian Prints

5 minutes Christmas Devotionals for Kids 2024

A 31-Day Inspirational Journey for Children, Plus Winter Wonder Family Games and Bonding Moments

Jeremiah Christian Prints

Copyright

Copyright © 2024 [Jeremiah Christian Prints]. All rights reserved.

No part of this publication may be reproduced, distributed, or transmitted in any form or by any means, including photocopying, recording, or other electronic or mechanical methods, without the prior written permission of the publisher, except in the case of brief quotations embodied in critical reviews and certain other non-commercial uses permitted by copyright law.

Scripture quotations are taken from the Holy Bible, New International Version® (NIV).

This book is a work of non-fiction. Any references to real people, events, or locales are used factually. Any resemblance to other events or persons, living or dead, is purely coincidental. The publisher has taken reasonable measures to ensure the accuracy of the information presented in this book. However, neither the author nor the publisher assumes any responsibility for errors, omissions, or contrary interpretations of the subject matter herein.

Table of Content

5 minutes Christmas Devotionals for Kids 2024 3
Copyright 5
Table of Content 7
Introduction 1
Week 1: Preparing Our Hearts for Christmas.. 7
Day 1 8
The Countdown Begins: Getting Ready for Christmas in Our Hearts 8
Day 2 11
God's Promise of a Savior: The Prophets' Message of Hope 11
Day 3 14
A King Like No Other: Jesus, Our Humble King 14
Day 4 17
The Angel's Visit to Mary: A Special Message from Heaven 17
Day 5 20
Mary's Faithful Heart: Trusting God's Big Plans 20
Day 6 23
Joseph's Dream: Joseph's Obedience to God 23
Day 7 26

The Journey to Bethlehem: The Long Road to Jesus' Birthplace...................... 26
Week 2: The Miracle of Jesus' Birth................... 29
Day 8... 30
No Room in the Inn: Finding a Place for Jesus.. 30
Day 9... 33
The Birth of Jesus: A Savior is Born in a Manger... 33
Day 10... 36
The Angels' Song: Celebrating Jesus' Birth with the Angels.. 36
Day 11... 39
The Shepherds' Surprise: Hearing the Good News from Heaven.. 39
Day 12... 42
Sharing the Good News: The Shepherds Spread the Joy of Jesus...................................... 42
Day 13... 45
The Star of Bethlehem: God's Special Light in the Sky... 45
Day 14... 48
The Wise Men Follow the Star: Seeking the Newborn King.. 48
Week 3: The Gifts and Joy of Christmas.......... 51
Day 15... 52
Gifts Fit for a King: The Wise Men's Gifts to Baby Jesus... 52
Day 16... 55

Jesus, the Greatest Gift: Why Jesus is God's Gift to Us..55
Day 17..58
God's Plan for Us: Trusting in God's Perfect Plan...58
Day 18..61
Mary's Song of Joy: Singing Praises to God Like Mary..61
Day 19..64
Joseph's Bravery: Being Brave Like Joseph in Following God...64
Day 20..67
The Stable's Special Night: A Humble Place for the King of Kings..67
Day 21..70
The Joy of Giving: Giving to Others Like Jesus Gave to Us...70
Week 4: The Love and Light of Christmas....73
Day 22..74
God's Love for Everyone: Christmas is for All People..74
Day 23..77
Christmas Around the World: How People Everywhere Celebrate Jesus....................................77
Day 24..80
The Night Before Christmas: Preparing Our Hearts for Jesus' Birth...80
Day 25..83
Jesus is Born!: Celebrating the Birth of Our

Savior..83
Day 26..86
The Blessing of Family: Thanking God for Our Families..86
Day 27..89
Jesus, the Light of the World: Letting Jesus' Light Shine Through Us..89
Day 28: Sharing Jesus' Love: Spreading Kindness and Love Like Jesus..92
Week 5: Keeping Christmas in Our Hearts..95
Day 29..97
The Spirit of Christmas—Keeping Christmas in Our Hearts All Year..97
Day 30..100
The Gift of Peace—Bringing God's Peace into the World..100
Day 31..103
Looking Forward to Jesus—Hope for the New Year and Jesus' Return..103
Conclusion..106
Carrying Christmas in Our Hearts All Year Long..106

Introduction

Welcome to **A Christmas Journey with Jesus**, a special devotional just for you! Christmas is one of the most exciting times of the year, but do you know why we celebrate it? It's not just about the gifts, decorations, and yummy food—it's about the greatest gift ever given: Jesus! This book will take you on a fun and meaningful journey, day by day, as we prepare our hearts to celebrate the birth of our Savior.

Through these pages, you will discover the miracles, joy, and love of Christmas in a way that's easy to understand and full of wonder. We'll learn about the people in the Bible who were part of the first Christmas, explore the exciting events surrounding Jesus' birth, and most importantly, grow closer to God as we look forward to celebrating the arrival of Jesus!

Each day, we'll read a special Bible verse, think about what it means in our lives, and say a simple prayer. Plus, you'll get to play fun games that help remind us of the wonder of Christmas! So grab your Bible, your favorite cozy spot, and let's take this Christmas journey together!

How to Use This Devotional

This devotional is designed to make each day leading up to Christmas—and a little beyond—extra special. Here's how to use it:

1. **Read the Bible Verse**
   Each day begins with a Bible verse that connects to the story of Jesus' birth. It's a good idea to read the verse aloud and think about what it means. You can ask your parents or siblings to join you in reading it too!
2. **Reflection**
   After reading the Bible verse, there's a reflection to help you understand the story better and connect it to your life. These reflections are written in a way that's easy to understand and full of fun examples. Take your time and think about how these stories apply to your day-to-day life. You'll see how Jesus' story isn't just for long ago—it's for right now!

3. **Questions to Think About**
   Every day, you'll find two questions that help you relate the lesson to real life. You can think about these questions on your own or talk about them with your family. They are meant to help you grow in your faith and see how you can be more like Jesus.
4. **Say a Prayer**
   At the end of each day, there is a short prayer to help you talk to God. You can say it out loud or quietly in your heart. This prayer is a way to thank God for the lesson and to ask Him to help you follow Him each day.
5. **The Wonder of Christmas: A Fun Activity**
   Christmas is a time of joy and celebration, so every day includes a fun, easy-to-do indoor game or activity that helps you remember the day's lesson. These games are simple and don't need a lot of materials, so you can play them with your family or friends. They're designed to help you experience the wonder of Christmas in a joyful way!
6. **Weekly Themes**
   The devotional is split into five weeks,

each with its own theme. You'll focus on a different part of the Christmas story and what it means for us today. Here's a breakdown of the weekly themes:

- **Week 1: The Promise of Christmas** (December 1–7)
  We begin by learning about the promise of Jesus and how God prepared the world for His arrival.
- **Week 2: The Miracle of Jesus' Birth** (December 8–14)
  This week, we focus on the wonderful miracle of Jesus being born in a stable.
- **Week 3: The Gifts and Joy of Christmas** (December 15–21)
  As we get closer to Christmas, we'll think about the wise men's gifts and the joy Jesus brings to us all.
- **Week 4: The Love and Light of Christmas** (December 22–28)
  This week is all about God's love and the light Jesus brings into our lives and the world.
- **Week 5: Keeping Christmas in Our Hearts** (December 29–31)

Even after Christmas is over, we can keep the joy, love, and hope of Christmas in our hearts all year long.

Special Tips for Using This Devotional:

- **Set a Special Time:** Pick a quiet time each day to do your devotional. It could be in the morning, before bed, or whenever you feel most peaceful.
- **Invite Your Family:** Ask your family to join you! Reading the Bible and learning about Jesus together makes Christmas even more special.
- **Have Fun with the Games:** Don't forget to play the "Wonder of Christmas" games. They are there to help you have fun while learning more about Jesus!
- **Pray from Your Heart:** Feel free to add your own thoughts and words to the prayers. Jesus loves hearing from you in your own special way.
- **Look for Jesus in Every Day:** As you go through each day, try to remember the lessons and see how you can follow Jesus in your actions, words, and thoughts.

I'm so excited to take this Christmas journey with you! Let's celebrate the birth of Jesus together, with joy, love, and fun, as we grow closer to Him. Merry Christmas!

Week 1: Preparing Our Hearts for Christmas

(December 1 - December 7)

As we begin this special month of December, we're getting ready to celebrate the amazing gift of Christmas! This week, we'll focus on preparing our hearts to welcome Jesus with love and joy. Just like we get our homes ready with decorations and Christmas lights, we also want to get our hearts ready by being kind, loving, and thankful. Each day, we'll explore how to follow Jesus' example and make this Christmas season extra special by filling our hearts with His love. Let's start our journey with excitement and open hearts as we get ready for the best Christmas ever!

Day 1

The Countdown Begins: Getting Ready for Christmas in Our Hearts

But when the set time had fully come, God sent his Son, born of a woman, born under the law.
— Galatians 4:4 (NIV)

Reflection:
Christmas is almost here, and the countdown has begun! But before we open presents or sing carols, the most important thing we need to do is get our hearts ready for Jesus. Christmas is His birthday, and we celebrate it because Jesus is the best gift ever! He came to show us God's love and to be our Savior.

Just like we decorate our homes and put up Christmas lights, we can decorate our hearts too! We do this by being kind, loving others, and spending time with God. When we fill our hearts with love, we're making a special place for Jesus.

As we count down the days to Christmas, let's remember that it's not just about gifts and treats. It's about celebrating Jesus, who came to show us the way to God. Each day, let's make sure our hearts are shining bright with love for Him and others!

Questions:

1. What is one thing you can do today to make your heart ready for Jesus?
2. Who can you show kindness to this Christmas season, just like Jesus shows kindness to you?

Prayer:
Dear Jesus, help me fill my heart with love and kindness as I get ready to celebrate Your birthday. Amen.

The Wonder of Christmas: Game - "Christmas Memory Match"

Let's play a fun game called **Christmas Memory Match!** Here's how to play:

- You'll need some small pieces of paper or cards. On half of them, draw a Christmas picture (like a tree, star, present, or angel), and on the other half, draw the same picture again to make a matching pair.
- Mix all the cards and lay them face down on a table.
- Each player takes turns flipping over two cards, trying to find a match. If the cards match, you get to keep them. If they don't match, turn them back over and let the next player have a turn.
- The player with the most matches at the end wins!

Day 2

God's Promise of a Savior: The Prophets' Message of Hope

The people walking in darkness have seen a great light; on those living in the land of deep darkness a light has dawned.
— Isaiah 9:2 (NIV)

Reflection:
A long time ago, before Jesus was born, God made a very special promise. He promised to send a Savior to the world to bring hope and light. This promise was told by prophets, people who listened to God and shared His messages. The prophets gave the people hope that even in dark times, a Savior would come to rescue them.

Can you imagine waiting for such an amazing promise to come true? The people waited for many years, but they never lost hope. They knew God always keeps His promises, and they trusted that one day the Savior would come. And guess what? That

Savior is Jesus, and He was born at Christmas to bring God's love to the whole world!

Just like the people long ago waited for Jesus, we get to celebrate that He is here! Every Christmas, we remember that God sent Jesus to be our Savior, and we can have hope because of Him. No matter what happens, Jesus is the light that shines in our hearts and helps us every day.

Questions:

1. What is something you've waited for that made you feel excited when it finally came?
2. How does Jesus bring hope and light into your life, just like He did for the people long ago?

Prayer:
Dear God, thank You for keeping Your promise and sending Jesus to be our Savior. Amen.

The Wonder of Christmas: Game - "Christmas I Spy"

Let's play a fun game called **Christmas I Spy!** Here's how to play:

- One person picks an object in the room related to Christmas (like a stocking, tree ornament, or candy cane) and says, "I spy with my little eye something that is [color, shape, or size]."
- The other players take turns guessing what the object is based on the clue.
- The first person to guess correctly gets to be the next one to spy something!

Day 3

A King Like No Other: Jesus, Our Humble King

For even the Son of Man did not come to be served, but to serve, and to give his life as a ransom for many.
— Mark 10:45 (NIV)

Reflection:
When we think of a king, we might picture someone wearing a crown, living in a big castle, and having lots of servants. But Jesus is a different kind of king. He didn't come to be rich or powerful in the way we might expect. Instead, He was born in a small, simple stable with animals all around Him. He came not to be served but to serve others.

Jesus showed us what true greatness looks like. It's not about having the most or being the most important person. It's about helping others, loving them, and being humble. Even though Jesus was God's Son and the King of the world, He was kind to everyone—especially those who needed help.

As we celebrate Christmas, let's remember that Jesus is a king who loves us deeply and came to serve us. We can be like Jesus by showing kindness to others and remembering that true greatness comes from loving and serving, just as He did.

Questions:

1. How can you show kindness and serve others like Jesus, even in small ways?
2. What is something special you can do this Christmas to help someone who might need extra love or care?

Prayer:
Dear Jesus, thank You for being a humble king who came to love and serve us. Help me be kind and loving like You. Amen.

The Wonder of Christmas: Game - "Christmas Charades"

Let's play a fun game called **Christmas Charades!** Here's how to play:

- One person thinks of something related to Christmas (like decorating the tree, building a snowman, or wrapping presents) but doesn't say it out loud.
- Without talking, they act it out using their hands, face, and body while the others try to guess what they're doing.
- The first person to guess correctly gets to go next and act out something fun for everyone to guess!

Day 4

The Angel's Visit to Mary: A Special Message from Heaven

But the angel said to her, 'Do not be afraid, Mary; you have found favor with God. You will conceive and give birth to a son, and you are to call him Jesus.
— Luke 1:30-31 (NIV)

Reflection:
One day, something amazing happened to a young girl named Mary. An angel from heaven came to visit her with a very special message. The angel told her that she would have a baby, and that baby would be God's Son, Jesus! At first, Mary was surprised and a little scared. But the angel told her not to be afraid because God had chosen her for something wonderful.

Even though Mary didn't fully understand what was happening, she trusted God's plan. She knew that God loved her and that

He had an important job for her. Mary's heart was full of faith and courage as she accepted the angel's message.

Like Mary, sometimes God asks us to do things that may seem hard or scary, but we can trust that He will always help us. When we listen to God and follow Him, we're part of His great plan, just like Mary was when she said yes to being the mother of Jesus.

Questions:

1. How do you think Mary felt when the angel told her God's big plan for her?
2. Can you think of a time when you needed to trust God, even if you were a little scared or unsure?

Prayer:
Dear God, help me trust You, just like Mary did, and follow Your plans with a brave heart. Amen.

The Wonder of Christmas: Game - "Christmas Pictionary"

Let's play **Christmas Pictionary!** Here's how to play:

- One person thinks of a Christmas-related word (like "angel," "shepherd," or "Christmas tree") and then draws it on a piece of paper without talking.
- The others have to guess what is being drawn.
- The first person to guess correctly gets to draw the next Christmas picture!

Day 5

Mary's Faithful Heart: Trusting God's Big Plans

"I am the Lord's servant," Mary answered. "May your word to me be fulfilled." Then the angel left her.
— Luke 1:38 (NIV)

Reflection:
Mary was a young woman with a big heart full of faith. When the angel told her she would be the mother of Jesus, she had to trust that God had a wonderful plan for her life. Even though she didn't know exactly how everything would work out, Mary said yes to God's plan with a heart full of trust and hope.

It's not always easy to trust God, especially when we don't understand everything that's happening around us. But Mary showed us how to have a faithful heart by believing that God knows what's best for us. She trusted God's big plan even though it was something she couldn't completely see or understand.

As we think about Mary's story, let's remember that God has a special plan for each of us too. When we trust Him, even when things seem confusing or uncertain, we're showing faith just like Mary did. God loves us and wants to guide us, so we can trust Him with all our hearts.

Questions:

1. Can you think of a time when you had to trust God, even though you didn't understand what was happening?
2. How can you show faith in God's plans for you, just like Mary did?

Prayer:
Dear God, help me trust You with all my heart, even when I don't understand Your plans. Amen.

The Wonder of Christmas: Game - "Christmas Bingo"

Let's play **Christmas Bingo!** Here's how to play:

- Create bingo cards with different Christmas-themed pictures or words (like "snowman," "gift," or "reindeer"). You can make your own cards or print them out.
- As you call out each Christmas word or show the picture, players mark off the matching pictures or words on their cards.
- The first person to mark off a row, column, or diagonal shouts "Bingo!" and wins a small prize or a holiday treat.

Day 6

Joseph's Dream: Joseph's Obedience to God

"But after he had considered this, an angel of the Lord appeared to him in a dream and said, 'Joseph son of David, do not be afraid to take Mary home as your wife, because what is conceived in her is from the Holy Spirit.'"
— Matthew 1:20 (NIV)

Reflection:
Joseph was a good man who loved Mary very much. When he found out that Mary was going to have a baby, he was worried and didn't know what to do. But God sent an angel to visit him in a dream and told him not to be afraid. The angel explained that Mary's baby was very special—He was Jesus, the Son of God!

Even though Joseph didn't fully understand everything at first, he chose to trust God's message and be obedient. He listened to the angel and did exactly what God asked him to do. By following God's instructions, Joseph played an important role in bringing Jesus into the world.

Joseph's story teaches us that trusting and obeying God, even when we're unsure, is very important. Just like Joseph, we can listen to God and follow His guidance in our lives. When we trust God, we're part of His amazing plan, and He helps us do great things!

Questions:

1. Have you ever had to do something even though you were unsure or scared? How did you feel afterward?
2. How can you follow God's guidance in your daily life, just like Joseph did?

Prayer:
Dear God, help me listen to You and follow Your guidance, even when I'm unsure. Amen.

The Wonder of Christmas: Game - "Christmas Scavenger Hunt"

Let's play **Christmas Scavenger Hunt!** Here's how to play:

- Create a list of Christmas-themed items to find around the house (like a candy cane, a Christmas ornament, or a red sock).
- Hide these items in different places around the house.
- Give players the list and let them search for the items.
- The first person to find all the items on the list wins a small prize or a holiday treat.

Day 7

The Journey to Bethlehem: The Long Road to Jesus' Birthplace

"So Joseph also went up from the town of Nazareth in Galilee to Judea, to Bethlehem the town of David, because he belonged to the house and line of David."
— Luke 2:4 (NIV)

Reflection:
Mary and Joseph had a long journey ahead of them. They traveled all the way from their home in Nazareth to Bethlehem because the emperor wanted everyone to be counted. This was a very important trip because Bethlehem was where Jesus was going to be born. Even though the journey was hard, Mary and Joseph trusted that God had a special plan for them.

Imagine walking a really long way with only a donkey to help you carry your things! Mary and Joseph showed great courage and faith by making this journey. They knew that God had chosen them for something very special, and they were willing to go through difficulties to be part of His plan.

As we remember Mary and Joseph's journey, we can think about how we can trust God in our own lives. Even when things seem difficult or challenging, God is with us, guiding us and helping us along the way. Just like Mary and Joseph, we can be brave and keep our faith in God's wonderful plans.

Questions:

1. Can you think of a time when you had to go through something challenging but trusted God to help you?
2. How can you show courage and faith in your daily life, even when things are hard?

Prayer:
Dear God, help me trust You and be brave, just like Mary and Joseph, even when things are difficult. Amen.

The Wonder of Christmas: Game - "Christmas Obstacle Course"

Let's create a **Christmas Obstacle Course!** Here's how to play:

- Set up a fun obstacle course in your living room or a safe space using pillows, chairs, and other household items.
- Include challenges like crawling under a chair (like a tunnel), jumping over pillows (like hurdles), or balancing on a line of tape.
- Add Christmas-themed elements like decorating a small tree or carrying a "present" from one spot to another.
- Time each player as they complete the course and see who can finish the fastest!

Week 2: The Miracle of Jesus' Birth

(December 8 - December 14)

This week, we're celebrating the incredible miracle of Jesus' birth! From the amazing news that the angel gave to Mary and Joseph, to the special journey they made to Bethlehem, we'll learn about how God gave us the greatest gift ever—His Son, Jesus. Each day, we'll discover how this miraculous event brought hope and joy to the world. As we dive into the story of Jesus' birth, let's remember how amazing it is that God loves us so much and gave us the best Christmas present of all!

Day 8

No Room in the Inn: Finding a Place for Jesus

"While they were there, the time came for the baby to be born, and she gave birth to her firstborn, a son. She wrapped him in cloths and placed him in a manger, because there was no guest room available for them."
— Luke 2:6-7 (NIV)

Reflection:
When Mary and Joseph arrived in Bethlehem, they found that there was no room for them at the inn. They had to stay in a humble stable where animals were kept. Even though it wasn't a fancy place, it was the perfect spot for the most amazing event ever—Jesus being born! This teaches us that Jesus doesn't need fancy things to be happy; He just wants a special place in our hearts.

Just like there was no room in the inn for Jesus, sometimes our lives can get so busy that we forget to make time for Him. But Jesus wants to be close to us every day, not just during Christmas. We can always find a place for Him in our hearts, no matter what our days look like.

As we think about the humble stable where Jesus was born, let's remember to make room for Him in our lives. Whether it's through prayer, kindness, or spending time with family, we can always welcome Jesus into our hearts and show Him how much we care.

Questions:

1. How can you make time for Jesus in your daily routine, even when you're busy?
2. What is something special you can do to show Jesus that you're making room for Him in your heart?

Prayer:
Dear Jesus, help me make room for You in my heart every day and remember how special You are. Amen.

The Wonder of Christmas: Game - "Christmas Hide and Seek"

Let's play **Christmas Hide and Seek!** Here's how to play:

- Choose a Christmas-themed item (like a small ornament, a candy cane, or a festive toy) and hide it somewhere in the room.
- One person closes their eyes and counts to 20 while the others hide the item.
- After counting, the seeker tries to find the hidden item.
- The person who finds the item gets to be the next seeker.

Day 9

The Birth of Jesus: A Savior is Born in a Manger

"Today in the town of David a Savior has been born to you; he is the Messiah, the Lord. This will be a sign to you: You will find a baby wrapped in cloths and lying in a manger."
— Luke 2:11-12 (NIV)

Reflection:
On that very special night in Bethlehem, something wonderful happened—Jesus, the Savior of the world, was born! Even though He was the Son of God, He wasn't born in a grand palace but in a simple manger where animals ate. This shows us that Jesus came to be close to everyone, not just those who live in big houses.

Jesus' birth reminds us that God's love is for everyone. He came to bring hope and joy to all people, no matter where they are or what they have. By being born in a humble manger, Jesus showed that He values each of us and wants to be part of our lives, no matter how big or small our circumstances may be.

As we celebrate this amazing event, let's remember that Jesus came to be with us and loves us just as we are. We can show His love to others by being kind, caring, and sharing the joy of Christmas with everyone we meet.

Questions:

1. How does knowing that Jesus was born in a humble manger make you feel about His love for everyone?
2. What are some ways you can share the joy and love of Christmas with your friends and family?

Prayer:
Dear Jesus, thank You for coming to us in such a special way and showing us how much You love us. Help me share Your love with others. Amen.

The Wonder of Christmas: Game - "Christmas Memory Match"

Let's play **Christmas Memory Match**! Here's how to play:

- Create a set of Christmas-themed cards with pairs of matching pictures (like Santa, reindeer, ornaments, etc.).
- Shuffle the cards and lay them face down in a grid.
- Take turns flipping over two cards at a time to try to find matching pairs.
- If a match is found, keep the pair and take another turn. If not, turn the cards back over and let the next player go.
- The game continues until all the pairs are found. The player with the most pairs wins!

Day 10

The Angels' Song: Celebrating Jesus' Birth with the Angels

"Suddenly a great company of the heavenly host appeared with the angel, praising God and saying, 'Glory to God in the highest heaven, and on earth peace to those on whom his favor rests.'"
— Luke 2:13-14 (NIV)

Reflection:
When Jesus was born, the skies were filled with the most amazing music! Angels came down from heaven to sing a joyful song announcing Jesus' birth. They praised God and celebrated the wonderful news that Jesus had come to bring peace and love to the world. The angels' song was a way to share the happiness and excitement of this very special moment.

Imagine how incredible it must have been to hear all those angels singing! Their song reminds us how important and joyous

Jesus' birth is. Even though we can't hear the angels sing, we can still celebrate Jesus with our own joyful songs and praises.

As we think about the angels' song, let's find ways to celebrate Jesus in our own lives. Whether it's through singing Christmas carols, sharing kind words, or spending time with family, we can join in the celebration and spread the joy of Christmas just like the angels did.

Questions:

1. What are some ways you can celebrate Jesus' birth with joy and excitement in your daily life?
2. How can you share the happiness of Christmas with your friends and family?

Prayer:
Dear God, thank You for the angels who sang to celebrate Jesus' birth. Help me find joyful ways to celebrate and share Your love. Amen.

The Wonder of Christmas: Game - "Christmas Karaoke"

Let's have some fun with **Christmas Karaoke**! Here's how to play:

- Choose your favorite Christmas songs or carols.
- Take turns singing the songs, either solo or with friends and family.
- You can use a karaoke machine if you have one or just sing along to the music playing from a device.
- For added fun, dress up in festive costumes or use Christmas-themed props.

Day 11

The Shepherds' Surprise: Hearing the Good News from Heaven

"And there were shepherds living out in the fields nearby, keeping watch over their flocks at night. An angel of the Lord appeared to them, and the glory of the Lord shone around them, and they were terrified."
— Luke 2:8-9 (NIV)

Reflection:
Imagine being a shepherd out in the fields at night, just taking care of your sheep, when suddenly an angel appears! That's exactly what happened to the shepherds. They were very surprised and a bit scared, but the angel had some incredible news: Jesus, the Savior, was born! The angel told them that this was a joyous event for everyone and that they could find the baby wrapped in clothes and lying in a manger.

The shepherds were excited and amazed. They decided to go see Jesus for themselves and share the wonderful news with others. Their response teaches us that when we hear about something as amazing as Jesus' birth, it's worth celebrating and sharing with others. We can be like the shepherds by sharing the joy of Christmas and the good news about Jesus with our friends and family.

As we think about the shepherds' surprise, let's remember to be excited about the good news of Jesus and look for ways to share His love and joy with others. Just like the shepherds, we can spread the happiness of Christmas far and wide.

Questions:

1. How do you feel when you hear exciting news, and how can you share that excitement with others?
2. What are some ways you can share the joy of Jesus' birth with your friends and family?

Prayer:
Dear God, thank You for the wonderful news of Jesus' birth. Help me share this joy and excitement with everyone I meet. Amen.

The Wonder of Christmas: Game - "Christmas Bingo"

Let's play **Christmas Bingo**! Here's how to play:

- Create Bingo cards with Christmas-themed pictures or words (like a Christmas tree, snowman, gift, etc.).
- Write each picture or word on a card and make several copies.
- Use small pieces of paper or coins as markers.
- Call out the Christmas-themed words or show the pictures one at a time.
- Players mark off the items on their cards as they are called. The first person to complete a line (horizontally, vertically, or diagonally) shouts "Bingo!" and wins a small prize.

Day 12

Sharing the Good News: The Shepherds Spread the Joy of Jesus

"When they had seen him, they spread the word concerning what had been told them about this child, and all who heard it were amazed at what the shepherds said to them."
— Luke 2:17-18 (NIV)

Reflection:
After the shepherds visited Jesus, they couldn't keep the amazing news to themselves. They ran back to their fields, excitedly sharing what they had seen and heard with everyone they met. They told everyone about the special baby born in a manger and how the angels had announced His arrival. Their joy and excitement were contagious, and everyone was amazed at the wonderful news.

The shepherds showed us how important it is to share the good news about Jesus with others. When we learn something great, like the story of Jesus' birth, it's wonderful to tell others so they can share in the joy too. Just like the shepherds, we can spread happiness and share the love of Jesus with our friends, family, and everyone around us.

As we think about how the shepherds spread the joy of Jesus, let's look for ways to share the love and excitement of Christmas with those around us. By sharing the good news, we help others experience the joy and peace that comes from knowing Jesus.

Questions:

1. How can you share the joy of Christmas with your friends and family?
2. What are some ways you can tell others about Jesus and the special gift He is?

Prayer:
Dear Jesus, thank You for the amazing news of Your birth. Help me share Your love and joy with everyone around me. Amen.

The Wonder of Christmas: Game - "Christmas Charades"

Let's play **Christmas Charades**! Here's how to play:

- Write down different Christmas-themed activities or characters on small pieces of paper (like decorating a tree, Santa coming down the chimney, making cookies, etc.).
- Players take turns drawing a paper and acting out the activity or character without using words.
- The other players try to guess what is being acted out.
- The player who guesses correctly gets to go next.

Day 13

The Star of Bethlehem: God's Special Light in the Sky

"After Jesus was born in Bethlehem in Judea, during the time of King Herod, Magi from the east came to Jerusalem and asked, 'Where is the one who has been born king of the Jews? We saw his star when it rose and have come to worship him.'"
— Matthew 2:1-2 (NIV)

Reflection:
One of the most magical parts of the Christmas story is the shining star that appeared in the sky to guide the Wise Men to Jesus. This star was no ordinary star; it was a special light from God that showed the way to the new King. The Wise Men followed this bright star across the desert, knowing it would lead them to something wonderful.

The star of Bethlehem reminds us that God provides guidance and light in our lives, especially when we need it the most. Just like the star helped the Wise Men find Jesus, God's light helps us find our way and leads us to love and truth. When we trust in God, He will guide us through the darkness and help us find the way to His love and joy.

As we think about the star of Bethlehem, let's remember that God's light is always shining in our lives. We can follow His guidance by being kind, loving, and helping others, just as the Wise Men followed the star to find Jesus.

Questions:

1. How can you follow God's light and guidance in your daily life?
2. What are some ways you can be a "light" for others and help them find joy and love?

Prayer:
Dear God, thank You for the shining star that guided the Wise Men to Jesus. Help me follow Your light and share Your love with others. Amen.

The Wonder of Christmas: Game - "Star Scavenger Hunt"

Let's play **Star Scavenger Hunt**! Here's how to play:

- Create a list of small star-shaped items or Christmas-themed objects to find around the house (like star stickers, star ornaments, or toy stars).
- Hide these items in different places around the room or house.
- Give the players clues or a map to help them find the hidden stars.
- The first person or team to find all the stars wins a small prize.

Day 14

The Wise Men Follow the Star: Seeking the Newborn King

"When they saw the star, they were overjoyed. On coming to the house, they saw the child with his mother Mary, and they bowed down and worshiped him. Then they opened their treasures and presented him with gifts of gold, frankincense, and myrrh."
— Matthew 2:10-11 (NIV)

Reflection:
The Wise Men saw a bright star shining in the sky and knew it was a special sign from God. They traveled a long distance, following the star, to find the newborn King, Jesus. When they finally arrived, they were filled with joy and awe. They brought precious gifts to honor Jesus and showed their deep respect and love for Him.

The Wise Men's journey reminds us that seeking Jesus is worth every effort. They followed the star with great hope and faith, and their journey led them to a wonderful meeting with Jesus. It teaches us that when we seek Jesus with our whole hearts, we will find Him and experience His love and joy.

As we think about the Wise Men's adventure, let's remember to seek Jesus in our lives every day. We can follow His guidance, share His love with others, and find joy in the journey of knowing Him better.

Questions:

1. What are some ways you can seek Jesus in your daily life?
2. How can you show your love and respect for Jesus, just like the Wise Men did?

Prayer:
Dear Jesus, thank You for the Wise Men who followed the star to find You. Help me seek You with all my heart and share Your love with others. Amen.

The Wonder of Christmas: Game - "Christmas Star Search"

Let's play **Christmas Star Search!** Here's how to play:

- Hide star-shaped stickers or cutouts around a room or the house.
- Give players a set amount of time to find as many stars as they can.
- For added fun, you can have clues or hints leading to where some of the stars are hidden.
- The player who finds the most stars or finds all the hidden stars wins a small prize.

Week 3: The Gifts and Joy of Christmas

(December 15 - December 21

Welcome to Week 3, where we'll explore the wonderful gifts and joy that Christmas brings! During this week, we'll discover how the Wise Men brought special gifts to Jesus and how we can celebrate the joy of giving and receiving. Christmas is not just about the presents we unwrap but about the love and happiness we share with others. As we learn about the gifts given to Jesus, we'll also think about the most special gift of all—Jesus Himself—and how we can spread His love and joy through our own actions. Get ready for a week full of fun activities, heartwarming stories, and the true spirit of Christmas!

Day 15

Gifts Fit for a King: The Wise Men's Gifts to Baby Jesus

"Then they opened their treasures and presented him with gifts of gold, frankincense, and myrrh."
— Matthew 2:11 (NIV)

Reflection:
When the Wise Men arrived at Jesus' birthplace, they brought very special gifts: gold, frankincense, and myrrh. Each of these gifts was chosen with great care. Gold was a precious metal that showed Jesus was a King. Frankincense was a fragrant incense used in worship, showing that Jesus was worthy of praise. Myrrh was a special spice used for preparing bodies, which reminded everyone of the great sacrifice Jesus would make.

The Wise Men's gifts teach us that giving something thoughtful and meaningful is a wonderful way to show love. They didn't just bring any gifts—they chose what was most precious to them to honor Jesus. This reminds us that we can also give our best gifts, not just on Christmas, but all year round, to show our love for Jesus and others.

As we think about the gifts the Wise Men brought, let's also think about how we can give our best gifts of love, kindness, and joy to those around us, just like the Wise Men did for Jesus.

Questions:

1. What are some thoughtful ways you can show love to your family and friends?
2. How can you make your gifts or actions special and meaningful, just like the Wise Men did?

Prayer:
Dear Jesus, thank You for the wonderful gifts the Wise Men brought You. Help me give my best gifts of love and kindness to others. Amen.

The Wonder of Christmas: Game - "Gift Wrap Relay"

Let's play **Gift Wrap Relay**! Here's how to play:

- Divide players into teams and give each team some wrapping paper, tape, and ribbons.
- Each team must race to wrap a "gift" (a small box or object) as neatly as possible.
- Once wrapped, they pass the gift to the next team member, who must add a ribbon or bow.
- The first team to finish wrapping their gift and decorating it wins a small prize.

Day 16

Jesus, the Greatest Gift: Why Jesus is God's Gift to Us

"For God so loved the world that he gave his one and only Son, that whoever believes in him shall not perish but have eternal life."
— John 3:16 (NIV)

Reflection:
Christmas is such a special time because we celebrate the greatest gift of all: Jesus! God gave us Jesus because He loves us so much. Jesus is not just any gift; He is the best gift because He brings us hope, joy, and the promise of eternal life with God. When we think about gifts, we often think of toys or presents, but Jesus is a gift that fills our hearts with love and peace.

Jesus came to Earth as a baby to show us how much God loves us and to teach us how to live in love and kindness. By coming into the world, Jesus made it possible for us to have a close relationship with God. This is the most amazing gift we could ever receive, and it's one we can cherish every day of our lives.

As we celebrate Christmas, let's remember that Jesus is the best gift we could ever receive. We can show our thanks by sharing His love with others and living in a way that honors Him.

Questions:

1. What are some ways you can show gratitude for the gift of Jesus in your daily life?
2. How can you share the love and joy of Jesus with your friends and family?

Prayer:
Dear God, thank You for the incredible gift of Jesus. Help me share His love and joy with everyone I meet. Amen.

The Wonder of Christmas: Game - "Christmas Gift Bingo"

Let's play **Christmas Gift Bingo!** Here's how to play:

- Create Bingo cards with Christmas-themed pictures or words in each square (like a Christmas tree, gift, candy cane, etc.).
- Use small items or stickers to mark off the squares as you call out the items.
- The first player to get a line of marked squares (horizontally, vertically, or diagonally) shouts "Bingo!" and wins a small prize.

Day 17

God's Plan for Us: Trusting in God's Perfect Plan

"For I know the plans I have for you," declares the Lord, "plans to prosper you and not to harm you, plans to give you a hope and a future."
— Jeremiah 29:11 (NIV)

Reflection:
Have you ever wondered what plans God has for you? Just like He had a special plan when He sent Jesus to be born in Bethlehem, He has a wonderful plan for each one of us. God's plan for our lives is full of love and hope, even if we don't always understand it. When things get tough or confusing, we can trust that God is guiding us and working everything out for our good.

The story of Christmas is a beautiful reminder that God's plans are always perfect. He planned for Jesus to come into the world to save us and bring us closer to

Him. When we trust in God's plan, we can feel safe knowing that He is always looking out for us and wants what's best for us.

This Christmas, let's remember to trust in God's plan for our lives. No matter what happens, we can be sure that God is with us, guiding us, and helping us to grow in His love and grace.

Questions:

1. How can you trust God's plan when things don't go the way you expect?
2. What are some ways you can look for signs of God's plan and trust that He is guiding you?

Prayer:
Dear God, thank You for Your perfect plan for my life. Help me trust in You and follow Your guidance every day. Amen.

The Wonder of Christmas: Game - "God's Plan Puzzle"

Let's play **God's Plan Puzzle**! Here's how to play:

- Create or print out a simple Christmas-themed puzzle with a picture or message about trusting God's plan.
- Cut the puzzle into pieces and mix them up.
- Let the players work together to put the puzzle back together, talking about how trusting God's plan can help us in different situations.
- The first team to complete the puzzle wins a small prize.

Day 18

Mary's Song of Joy: Singing Praises to God Like Mary

"My soul glorifies the Lord and my spirit rejoices in God my Savior."
— Luke 1:46-47 (NIV)

Reflection:
Mary was filled with joy and gratitude when she learned she would be the mother of Jesus. Her heart overflowed with praise for God, and she sang a beautiful song called the Magnificat. Mary's song was a way of celebrating how amazing and loving God is. She was excited to be part of God's big plan and wanted to share her happiness with everyone.

Mary's example teaches us that we can sing and praise God too, not just during Christmas, but every day. Even when things are challenging, we can find reasons to celebrate God's love and goodness. Singing praises helps us remember how wonderful

God is and reminds us to be thankful for all the blessings we have.

This Christmas, let's follow Mary's example and sing joyful songs to God. It's a special way to express our love and appreciation for all that He has done for us and to share that joy with others.

Questions:

1. How can you show your joy and thankfulness to God in your daily life?
2. What are some of your favorite songs that help you feel close to God and celebrate His love?

Prayer:
Dear God, thank You for the joy and love You bring into our lives. Help me sing praises to You with a joyful heart, just like Mary did. Amen.

The Wonder of Christmas: Game - "Christmas Karaoke"

Let's play **Christmas Karaoke!** Here's how to play:

- Choose a few popular Christmas songs and find the lyrics.
- Take turns singing the songs with the lyrics or using a karaoke machine if you have one.
- Encourage everyone to sing their hearts out and have fun.
- You can even have a little prize for the best performance or the most enthusiastic singer.

Day 19

Joseph's Bravery: Being Brave Like Joseph in Following God

"When Joseph woke up, he did what the angel of the Lord had commanded him and took Mary home as his wife."
— Matthew 1:24 (NIV)

Reflection:
Joseph was a very brave man. When he learned that Mary was going to have a baby, he didn't know what to do. But when an angel told him it was part of God's plan, Joseph trusted God and chose to be brave. He took Mary as his wife and helped take care of her and baby Jesus, even though it wasn't an easy thing to do.

Joseph's bravery teaches us that following God's plans can sometimes be hard or confusing, but it's always the right thing to do. Just like Joseph trusted and obeyed God, we can be brave in following God's guidance in our lives. Being brave means trusting God even when we don't understand everything.

This Christmas, let's remember Joseph's bravery and find ways to be brave in our own lives. Whether it's standing up for what is right or helping others, we can follow Joseph's example and trust God with courage.

Questions:

1. Can you think of a time when you needed to be brave, just like Joseph? How did you handle it?
2. How can you show bravery and trust in God when you face difficult or new situations?

Prayer:
Dear God, thank You for Joseph's bravery and trust in You. Help me to be brave and follow Your guidance in my own life. Amen.

The Wonder of Christmas: Game - "Brave Adventurers"

Let's play **Brave Adventurers!** Here's how to play:

- Set up a simple obstacle course or a series of challenges in your home using pillows, chairs, and other safe items.
- Have the kids complete the course, pretending they are brave adventurers like Joseph.
- You can add tasks like "rescue the teddy bear" or "cross the wobbly bridge" to make it more fun.
- Celebrate everyone's bravery and effort with small rewards or praise.

Day 20

The Stable's Special Night: A Humble Place for the King of Kings

"She wrapped him in cloths and placed him in a manger, because there was no guest room available for them."
— Luke 2:7 (NIV)

Reflection:
On the very first Christmas night, Jesus, the King of Kings, was born in a humble stable. This special place was not grand or fancy, but it was where Mary and Joseph welcomed their baby with love. Even though Jesus was the Son of God, He chose to come into the world in a simple manger, showing us that God values humility and love more than grand appearances.

The stable reminds us that Jesus' love is for everyone, no matter how big or small, rich or poor. It doesn't matter where we come from or what we have; what matters is the love we share and the kindness we show to others. This Christmas, let's remember that God's love can be found in the simplest and humblest of places.

As we celebrate Christmas, we can create our own special and humble moments by sharing our love with those around us. Just like the stable was special because of the love it held, our simple acts of kindness make our hearts and homes shine with God's love.

Questions:

1. How can you show love and kindness to others, even if you don't have a lot to give?
2. What are some small, humble ways you can make someone's Christmas special?

Prayer:
Dear God, thank You for coming to us in such a humble way. Help me to show Your love through my own simple acts of kindness and to cherish the true spirit of Christmas. Amen.

The Wonder of Christmas: Game - "Stable Decorators"

Let's play **Stable Decorators!** Here's how to play:

- Use paper, markers, and other craft supplies to create a simple stable scene.
- Have the kids decorate their "stable" with festive drawings, stickers, or other decorations.
- After decorating, talk about how the stable was a special place for Jesus and how we can make our own spaces warm and welcoming for others.

Day 21

The Joy of Giving: Giving to Others Like Jesus Gave to Us

"It is more blessed to give than to receive."
— Acts 20:35 (NIV)

Reflection:
Jesus gave us the most wonderful gift of all: His love and salvation. This Christmas, we remember how special it is to give to others, just like Jesus gave to us. When we give, whether it's a kind word, a helpful hand, or a special present, we're sharing the joy and love that Jesus shared with us.

Giving is not just about the presents we wrap; it's also about showing kindness and care. When we help others and share what we have, we spread happiness and show God's love in our own way. Every little act of giving makes a big difference and fills our hearts with joy.

So, this Christmas, let's find ways to give to others with a happy heart. Whether it's sharing a toy, making a card, or simply being a good friend, each act of kindness is a way to show how much we care and to celebrate the true spirit of Christmas.

Questions:

1. What is something kind you can do for someone else this Christmas?
2. How does it make you feel when you give something special to others?

Prayer:
Dear God, thank You for the gift of Jesus and for teaching us the joy of giving. Help me to share Your love with others through my own acts of kindness and generosity. Amen.

The Wonder of Christmas: Game - "Gift Givers Relay"

Let's play **Gift Givers Relay**! Here's how to play:

- Set up a relay race with a small gift or a wrapped box at the start line.

- Have the kids race to the gift, pick it up, and carry it carefully to a designated spot.
- After placing the gift, they run back to tag the next player.
- The game continues until everyone has had a turn, and then talk about how each player's effort helped "deliver" the gift.

Week 4: The Love and Light of Christmas

(December 22 - December 28)

As we enter the final week of December, we celebrate the Love and Light of Christmas. This week, we'll explore how Jesus, the Light of the World, brings warmth and joy to our hearts. Christmas is a special time when we remember how Jesus came to show us God's incredible love. Through His birth, we learn about the true meaning of love and how we can share that love with everyone around us. Let's focus on the bright light of Jesus' love and find ways to let it shine through us as we continue to celebrate this joyful season!

Day 22

God's Love for Everyone: Christmas is for All People

"For God so loved the world that he gave his one and only Son, that whoever believes in him shall not perish but have eternal life."
— John 3:16 (NIV)

Reflection:
Christmas is a wonderful time to remember that God's love is for everyone. No matter where we come from or who we are, God's love is always with us. Just like the shepherds and wise men came from different places to see baby Jesus, Christmas shows us that Jesus came for all people, everywhere.

Jesus' birth reminds us that we are all special to God. When we celebrate Christmas, we're not just celebrating a holiday; we're celebrating God's incredible love that includes everyone. This season is a perfect time to share that love with our friends, family, and neighbors.

As we enjoy the holiday season, let's remember to show kindness and love to everyone we meet. By sharing our joy and being friendly, we can help others feel the warmth of God's love, just like the first Christmas was filled with joy and wonder for all.

Questions:

1. How can you show love to someone who might not have many friends or family around during Christmas?
2. What are some ways you can make everyone feel included and special this holiday season?

Prayer:
Dear God, thank You for loving everyone and showing us that Christmas is for all people. Help me to share Your love with everyone around me and make everyone feel special this Christmas. Amen.

The Wonder of Christmas: Game - "Christmas Around the World"

Let's play **Christmas Around the World!** Here's how to play:

- Create simple cards with different countries and how they celebrate Christmas (like decorating with different colors, special foods, or traditions).
- Spread the cards around the room.
- Have the kids take turns picking a card, learning about the tradition, and then sharing it with the group.
- After learning about different traditions, have a group discussion about how each one reflects love and joy.

Day 23

Christmas Around the World: How People Everywhere Celebrate Jesus

"For we are all one in Christ Jesus."
— Galatians 3:28 (NIV)

Reflection:
Christmas is a special time when people all around the world celebrate the birth of Jesus in different and exciting ways. From snowy Christmas trees in the North to sunny beaches in the South, every country has its own special traditions to honor Jesus. Even though the celebrations might look different, the joy and love we feel for Jesus are the same everywhere.

In every corner of the globe, people light up their homes, sing songs, and gather with family and friends to remember the amazing gift of Jesus. This shows us that no matter where we are or what we do, we're all celebrating the same incredible gift—God's love through Jesus.

As we learn about how others celebrate, we see that Christmas brings us all together. It's a beautiful reminder that Jesus' love is for everyone, and it connects us all as one big family in Christ.

Questions:

1. What is a special Christmas tradition you have at home that you enjoy?
2. How do you think learning about other people's Christmas traditions can help us understand more about God's love?

Prayer:
Dear God, thank You for the many ways people celebrate Jesus around the world. Help me to appreciate and learn from these traditions and to share Your love with everyone I meet. Amen.

The Wonder of Christmas: Game - "Holiday Traditions Match-Up"
Let's play **Holiday Traditions Match-Up!** Here's how to play:

- Create cards with pictures and descriptions of different Christmas traditions from around the world.
- Shuffle and spread them out on the floor or a table.
- Have the kids take turns picking two cards to see if they match (e.g., a tradition with its country).
- Once a match is found, read about the tradition and discuss it as a group.

Day 24

The Night Before Christmas: Preparing Our Hearts for Jesus' Birth

"But the angel said to them, 'Do not be afraid. I bring you good news that will cause great joy for all the people. Today in the town of David a Savior has been born to you; he is the Messiah, the Lord.'"
— Luke 2:10-11 (NIV)

Reflection:
On the night before Christmas, we get ready to celebrate the birth of Jesus with excitement and joy. Just like Mary and Joseph prepared for the arrival of Jesus, we can prepare our hearts by thinking about how much Jesus loves us. It's a special time to reflect on what Christmas really means and how we can welcome Jesus into our lives.

As we get ready for Christmas, it's a perfect moment to remember that Jesus' birth is a gift of love for everyone. We can take a few quiet moments to think about the joy Jesus brings and how we can share that joy with others. It's not just about presents and decorations, but about feeling thankful for the greatest gift of all—Jesus.

So, let's fill our hearts with love and kindness as we celebrate Jesus' birth. This Christmas Eve, let's be like the shepherds and angels who were so excited to share the good news of Jesus' arrival with everyone around them.

Questions:

1. How can you prepare your heart to celebrate Jesus' birth this Christmas?
2. What are some ways you can show love and kindness to others as you celebrate Christmas?

Prayer:
Dear God, thank You for the special gift of Jesus. Help me to prepare my heart with love and joy as we celebrate His birth. Amen.

The Wonder of Christmas: Game - "Christmas Eve Candlelight"

Let's play **Christmas Eve Candlelight!** Here's how to play:

- Gather a few battery-operated candles or make paper candles with flashlight apps.
- Sit in a circle and pass the "candle" around while music plays softly.
- When the music stops, the person holding the candle shares one thing they are excited about for Christmas or a way they can show love to others.
- Continue until everyone has had a turn.

Day 25

Jesus is Born!: Celebrating the Birth of Our Savior

"Today in the town of David a Savior has been born to you; he is the Messiah, the Lord."
— Luke 2:11 (NIV)

Reflection:
Today is the most wonderful day of all because we celebrate the birth of Jesus, our Savior! Imagine the excitement in Bethlehem when Jesus was born—angels sang, shepherds came to see Him, and the whole world started to understand how much God loves us. Jesus came as a tiny baby, but He brought with Him a huge gift of love and hope for everyone.

As we celebrate, let's remember that Christmas is not just about gifts and decorations, but about the amazing gift of Jesus. He came to show us how much we are loved and to teach us how to love others. So, let's fill today with joy and thankfulness, just like the angels and shepherds did.

Take some time today to think about how you can share the joy of Jesus' birth with those around you. Whether it's through kind words, a hug, or a simple act of love, let's celebrate Jesus by showing love to others.

Questions:

1. How can you show the love of Jesus to your family and friends today?
2. What is one special way you can celebrate Jesus' birth with others?

Prayer:
Dear God, thank You for the wonderful gift of Jesus. Help me to celebrate His birth with joy and share His love with everyone I meet. Amen.

The Wonder of Christmas: Game - "Christmas Charades"
Let's play **Christmas Charades!** Here's how to play:

- Write down Christmas-themed words or phrases (like "decorating the tree," "singing carols," or "opening presents") on small pieces of paper and put them in a bowl.
- Take turns drawing a paper from the bowl and acting out the word or phrase without speaking.
- The rest of the group guesses what you're acting out. If they guess correctly, you get a point!

Day 26

The Blessing of Family: Thanking God for Our Families

"Honor your father and your mother, so that you may live long in the land the Lord your God is giving you."
— Exodus 20:12 (NIV)

Reflection:
Family is one of the most special gifts God gives us. Just like Mary, Joseph, and baby Jesus were a family, we have our own families to love and care for. God planned for families to be a place where we feel safe, loved, and supported. Our families might look different from one another, but God gave each of us a family to share His love with.

At Christmas, it's a great time to thank God for our families. We can show our love by being kind, sharing, and spending time together. Just like the shepherds went to see baby Jesus with joy, we can celebrate with our families, knowing that God has blessed us with them.

As we enjoy the holidays, let's remember to pray for our families and be grateful for every hug, smile, and moment spent together. Whether we're laughing, playing games, or eating a meal, we are celebrating the gift of family that God has given us.

Questions:

1. What is one thing you love about your family that you want to thank God for?
2. How can you show kindness and love to your family today?

Prayer:
Dear God, thank You for the blessing of my family. Help me show love and kindness to them every day. Amen.

The Wonder of Christmas: Game - "Family Memory Game"
Here's how to play **Family Memory Game:**

- Have each family member share one of their favorite memories from the past year.
- After each person shares, another family member tries to repeat the memory to see how well they remember!
- Take turns going around the room, sharing and repeating the special moments.

Day 27

Jesus, the Light of the World: Letting Jesus' Light Shine Through Us

"When Jesus spoke again to the people, he said, 'I am the light of the world. Whoever follows me will never walk in darkness, but will have the light of life.'"
— John 8:12 (NIV)

Reflection:
When Jesus was born, His light entered the world to guide us. Just like a bright star shining in the sky, Jesus' love shows us the way, even when things seem dark or scary. His light helps us make good choices, be kind to others, and share His love with everyone we meet.

We can let Jesus' light shine through us by doing good things like helping someone in need, being a good friend, or even just sharing a smile. When we follow Jesus, we become like little lights, spreading warmth and joy wherever we go. Just like a candle lights up a room, your kindness and love can light up someone's day.

This Christmas, think about how you can be a light for others. Whether it's sharing your toys, helping your parents, or comforting a friend, you're reflecting Jesus' light to the world. Every little act of kindness shows others the love of Jesus.

Questions:

1. How can you let Jesus' light shine through you this Christmas season?
2. Can you think of a time when someone's kindness made you feel happy? How did that show Jesus' love?

Prayer:
Jesus, help me to be a light in the world and share Your love with others. Amen.

The Wonder of Christmas: Game - "Light Up the Room"
Here's how to play **Light Up the Room:**

- In a darkened room, take turns pretending to be a "light" by doing a kind or helpful action.
- Every time someone acts like a "light," the room gets a little brighter by turning on one more small light or candle.
- Continue until the room is filled with light and love!

Day 28

Sharing Jesus' Love: Spreading Kindness and Love Like Jesus

"A new command I give you: Love one another. As I have loved you, so you must love one another."
— John 13:34 (NIV)

Reflection:
Jesus showed us how to love others by being kind, patient, and caring. He didn't just love His friends; He loved everyone, even people who others didn't treat kindly. This is the kind of love Jesus wants us to share too! When we love others like Jesus, we show the world what His love looks like.

You can share Jesus' love in simple ways—by being kind to your siblings, helping your parents, or giving someone a hug when they feel sad. Every act of love, no matter how small, shows that you care and that Jesus is working through you. Just like

Jesus loved everyone, we can spread kindness to everyone around us.

This Christmas season, remember that Jesus' love is the greatest gift we can share. As you celebrate with your family and friends, think about how you can spread that love and make someone's day a little brighter!

Questions:

1. How can you show love and kindness to someone in your family today?
2. Can you think of a time when someone was kind to you? How did it make you feel?

Prayer:
Dear Jesus, help me to love others like You do and share Your kindness with everyone. Amen.

The Wonder of Christmas: Game - "Pass the Love"
Here's how to play **Pass the Love:**

- Sit in a circle with your family or friends.
- One person starts by saying something kind or loving to the person next to them (like a compliment or a kind word).
- That person then "passes the love" by saying something kind to the next person, and it goes around the circle.
- Keep going and see how much love you can pass around!

Week 5: Keeping Christmas in Our Hearts

(December 29 - December 31)

As Christmas comes to an end, we don't have to say goodbye to the joy, love, and light it brings. Christmas isn't just about one day—it's about keeping the spirit of Jesus' love alive in our hearts all year long! We can carry the kindness, generosity, and peace we feel at Christmas into every day by remembering how Jesus was born to show us God's love. Let's promise to keep that love shining bright, not just during the holidays, but in everything we do, wherever we go!

Day 29

The Spirit of Christmas—Keeping Christmas in Our Hearts All Year

"Let us not become weary in doing good, for at the proper time we will reap a harvest if we do not give up."
—Galatians 6:9 (NIV)

Reflection:
Christmas is a time when everyone feels joyful, kind, and full of love. But did you know that we can keep the spirit of Christmas alive all year long? Just like how Jesus' love doesn't go away after December, we can continue to share kindness and spread joy every single day. The love, joy, and peace we feel at Christmas is a gift we can carry with us, no matter the season.

When we show love to others, help those in need, and say kind words, we are acting just like Jesus did. These actions make the world a little brighter, just like Christmas lights brighten up our homes. Even when it's not

Christmas, Jesus still wants us to share His love with the people around us.

So, even though the Christmas season comes and goes, the spirit of love and giving never has to stop. Imagine how happy we can make the world if we act like it's Christmas all year! By keeping the spirit of Christmas in our hearts, we honor Jesus every day.

Question:

1. How can you show kindness and love to someone in your family or at school, even when it's not Christmas?
2. What are some ways you can share the joy of Jesus with others all year long?

Prayer:
Dear Jesus, help me keep the spirit of Christmas in my heart every day. Amen.

The Wonder of Christmas: Indoor Game—Pass the Ornament
Gather everyone in a circle. One person starts by holding a soft ornament (or a

small, light object like a pillow). Play some Christmas music, and while the music plays, pass the ornament around the circle. When the music stops, whoever is holding the ornament must share one kind thing they can do for someone else that week. Continue the game until everyone has had a turn!

Day 30

The Gift of Peace—Bringing God's Peace into the World

"Blessed are the peacemakers, for they will be called children of God."
—Matthew 5:9 (NIV)

Reflection:
Peace is one of the greatest gifts that God gave us, and Jesus came to bring peace to the world. At Christmas, we celebrate that special gift of peace. But what does it mean to have peace? Peace means feeling calm inside, knowing that God is with us, and it also means helping others to feel calm and happy. We can be like Jesus when we share peace with the people around us, whether it's through kind words or by being helpful when someone is upset.

Imagine a world where everyone is kind, patient, and forgiving. That's the kind of peace God wants for us! It's not always easy, but when we trust in Jesus and follow His example, we can bring peace to our families, our schools, and our friends. Even when things don't go our way, we can pray and ask God for the strength to be peacemakers.

As you celebrate Christmas, remember that peace isn't just something for one season. We can share God's peace every day of the year by being kind, forgiving, and loving to others, just like Jesus taught us. You can be a peacemaker, too!

Question:

1. How can you bring peace to someone who might be feeling sad or upset?
2. What is one way you can be a peacemaker at home or at school this week?

Prayer:
Dear God, help me share Your peace with others, and let me be a peacemaker like Jesus. Amen.

The Wonder of Christmas: Indoor Game—Silent Night Pass

In this game, players sit in a circle and try to pass a small object like a stuffed animal or a pillow from one person to another—but there's a catch! The room has to be completely silent. The goal is to pass the object around the circle without making any noise. If someone makes a sound, the object goes back to the start! This game teaches patience and helps everyone practice bringing a sense of calm and peace to the room.

Day 31

Looking Forward to Jesus—Hope for the New Year and Jesus' Return

"For the grace of God has appeared that offers salvation to all people. It teaches us to say 'No' to ungodliness and worldly passions, and to live self-controlled, upright and godly lives in this present age, while we wait for the blessed hope—the appearing of the glory of our great God and Savior, Jesus Christ."
—Titus 2:11-13 (NIV)

Reflection:
As we end the year and look forward to a new one, we also look forward to the greatest hope we have—Jesus! He came as a baby on Christmas to save us, and He promised that one day He will return again. This promise gives us hope, not just for a new year, but for every day of our lives. When we trust in Jesus, we know that He is

always with us, guiding us and filling our hearts with love and joy.

Every new year is a fresh start, and it's a great time to think about how we can grow closer to Jesus. We can ask ourselves, "How can I be more like Him in the new year?" Maybe it's being kinder, more patient, or spending more time in prayer. No matter what challenges we face, we know that Jesus will help us because He loves us and He has a special plan for each of us.

While we celebrate the hope of a new year, we also remember the hope of Jesus' return. Just like the wise men followed the star to find Jesus, we follow His light in our hearts, waiting for the day He will come back. Until then, we can share His love and light with everyone we meet!

Question:

1. What is one thing you can do in the new year to grow closer to Jesus?
2. How does knowing that Jesus will return one day give you hope and peace?

Prayer:
Dear Jesus, thank You for giving me hope for the new year and for Your promise to return. Help me follow You always. Amen.

The Wonder of Christmas: Indoor Game—New Year's Hope Jar

For this activity, grab a jar or a box and some small pieces of paper. Everyone writes down one hope or prayer they have for the new year, folds the paper, and places it in the jar. Once everyone has added their hopes, you can take turns pulling them out and reading them aloud (if you want) or keep them as a special secret between you and God. This game helps kids think about their hopes and dreams and reminds them to pray for guidance from Jesus throughout the year!

Conclusion

Carrying Christmas in Our Hearts All Year Long

As we come to the end of **"A Christmas Journey with Jesus,"** let's take a moment to think about everything we've learned. We've heard the story of Jesus' birth, sung with the angels, marveled at the shining star, and walked with the wise men. Each day of this devotional has helped us understand that Christmas is not just a one-time celebration; it's a reminder of God's love for us, every single day of the year.

Even though the Christmas season will soon be over, the lessons we've discovered don't have to end. Jesus came to bring light, hope, and love into the world. We can continue to carry that light by loving others, being kind, and sharing the good news of Jesus. Just like the shepherds who spread the news of His birth, we can spread joy to everyone we meet.

No matter what time of year it is, the spirit of Christmas can live in your heart. When you help someone in need, when you forgive, or when you pray, you are bringing the love of Jesus into the world. Jesus was born to be our Savior, and He will always be with us, guiding us and giving us hope.

So, as you move forward, remember: the gifts of Christmas—love, joy, peace, and hope—are not just for December. They are for every day! Keep looking to Jesus, and let His light shine in your heart all year long.

Merry Christmas! And may God bless you always.

Made in the USA
Coppell, TX
08 December 2024

42053825R00085